'Today a spiritual search is compounded by physical roadblocks. Oguibe confronts them and describes them with visionary eloquence.'
- Chinua Achebe, author of *Things Fall Apart*

'An eloquent testimony to the agony, despondency and nostalgia that plague the poet in exile.'
- *West Africa*

'Oguibe is very confident, very accomplished... his free verse is nicely poised and polished, and the power of the poetry is admirable.'
- Judges of the Noma Awards for Publishing in Africa

ALSO BY THE AUTHOR

A Song from Exile
A Gathering Fear
Songs for Catalina
The Culture Game
God's Transistor Radio
Uzo Egonu: An African Artist in the West
Sojourners: An Anthology of New Writing by Africans in Britain
The Struggle for South Africa's Mind

OLU OGUIBE

I AM BOUND TO THIS LAND BY BLOOD

Collected Poems

Born in 1964, Olu Oguibe studied at the University of Nigeria from which he was briefly suspended as an undergraduate and eventually expelled as a graduate student, and London University where he received a doctoral degree in art history. He has taught in colleges and universities in Nigeria, the United Kingdom and the United States including University of South Florida where he held the Stuart Golding Endowed Chair in African Art, and University of Connecticut where he served as director of the Institute for African American Studies. In addition to poetry, Oguibe has published extensively as an art historian and theorist. He is also a practicing artist whose work has been widely exhibited in major museums and galleries around the world. Oguibe is a senior fellow of the Smithsonian Institution and was honored in 2013 with the State of Connecticut Governor's Award for excellence and lifetime achievement in the arts.

OLU OGUIBE

I AM BOUND TO THIS LAND BY BLOOD

COLLECTED POEMS

OLU OGUIBE

I AM BOUND TO THIS LAND BY BLOOD

COLLECTED POEMS

UHIE PAPERBACKS
Rockville

Some of the poems in this collection originally appeared in *West Africa* magazine, *Wasafiri, The Daily Times, The Guardian Literary Review*, different edited anthologies, and three previous collections, *A Song from Exile* published by Norbert Aas, 1990, *A Gathering Fear* published by Verlag Norbert Aas, 1992, and *Songs for Catalina* published by Savannah Gallery, London, 1994.

The text of this book is set in Adobe Garamond.
Book design by the author.
Cover image: "Horse and Bus", 1994 by Olu Oguibe
Author Photograph © Olu Oguibe

First published by Uhie in 2013
First edition

Uhie ISBN 978-0-9848695-1-0

Uhie
174 West Main Street
Rockville, CT 06066

Manufactured in the United States of America
Uhie Paperbacks are printed on acid free paper.

To the memory
of my little brother
Osinachi Oguibe
1976-1980

Contents

Author's Note

THE POEMS collected in this volume span twenty-five years of work, a good many of those years spent in exile. They include three previously published volumes: *A Song from Exile, A Gathering Fear*, and *Songs for Catalina*, as well as poems previously published in news dailies and literary journals, and others that appear here for the first time. Some of the poems I have altered slightly, but most appear in their original form. The more recent poems I have grouped under later verse. The goal is to make them all available in one convenient volume.

My thanks go to Norbert Aas, publisher of my first two collections and an enduring believer in my work. Thanks also to Widdup Coubagy and Kaye Whiteman who both published my work over the years, and to Ike Achebe and Ike Okonta, my closest and most scrupulous critics in the first few years of my venture into verse.

During a rather difficult period in my life and that of my country, poetry was the railing that I leaned on to steady my gait past sorrow and despair, toward knowledge and understanding. In the very structure of the verse; in the often-rambling and arbitrary nature of the lines and the chaotic and unruly punctuation, for instance, I tried to capture or, at the very least, approximate the occasional beauty yet inescapable dissonance of our predicament.

To all who may find substance in some of these lines, I would simply say, as did Robert Frost, that the aim was song.

OLU OGUIBE
January 2013

A SONG FROM EXILE

for Kelly Tucker

After flight, after departures
The flames of this mood
Intone our birth cries.

- Uche Nduka, "Bruises"

I

I stand at the gates
Stranger and outsider
I have journeyed away
From the sea into the desert
The charm has crossed rivers
The tongue is numb
The songster has journeyed
Without his voice

So, here I stand
In a strange land
Among a strange people
Lone rooster in the square

I stand at the gates
Cold and alone
With the soil of my land
In a leather amulet
With photos and the hair
Of the woman I loved

A coward fled home
And the battlefront

Here, in this lair
Away from the heat
From the cries of children
And the sorrow of widows
From the bleat of sheep
And the chirp of crickets
Hid from the wolves
And the hunting dog

Away from my mother

Far away even from
These vagabond streets
From the whisky and the rock
And the sweat of bodies
The blasphemies of whores
And the smoke of hashish

Here where the cold
Curdles the blood in my eyes
And stares brand my
Forehead like a slaveholder's
Iron, here, cold and alone
Drenched to the bone
With my rage and shame
I have only memory
To cuddle for warmth.

II

On the streets I
See my countrymen

In the pubs, in the parks
At the underground stations

At the post office, and they
Always hurry past

Some trotting like pigeons
With children by their side

Some, old and heavy
Shuffling with the pain of age

Some with the right accent
And salt on their tongues

Some others paling now
With jelly in their hair

And everyone hurries past
Hurrying, facing away

No words pass between
No sign of our common kin

No bows to a mother
No elder's blessing to a child

The blood erupts in me
Our blood, and I wonder:

These men and women
With their gazes to the ground

Do they also carry these
Needles in my heart?

III

Conscience makes my bed with a quilt of thorns
Ah! Conscience that leashes a man to his past

Conscience that stakes a man in the open
Courtyard and pelts him with rain

Conscience that strips a man in the marketplace
Conscience has taken a seat in my inner room

Conscience arraigns me before the gallery
Of men and calls me into question

And there is laughter in the hall
Conscience clings to my skin like cheap perfume

Conscience hangs around me like a prisoner's tag
And who says there is peace

Away from home?
Or honor

Or pride
Or a sense of clan?

Without conscience the exile is set adrift
Like cottonseed on the wings of the wind

A grain in the drifting sand dunes of the earth
He is like the waters of a river coursing endlessly

Through mountains and forests
Into the jaws of the sea where it is lost forever

Without conscience the exile
Is a blind, stomping masquerade

Lost abroad without his escorts
Ah! Conscience, the thug of the soul

Whoever is whole
Without his soul?

Conscience hedges me in like the edges of a lake
Conscience follows me like my mother's eyes

Conscience! This jeering
Torturer sitting by me.

IV

At night when the world is dead
And the sidewalks are free

Of the laughter of men
I walk the streets in my rage

False city! Dog city!
I curse this city and its name

And in the day when the sun is up
I walk the graveyards

Which faces here can tell
Sores the exile bears within?

Walls crumble here
But they are going up at home

And here the crowns are tumbling
But they grow thicker there

There is jubilation at my door
Bright flags ride the open air

Yet, I weep in my sleep
Which friend can share

In the exile's private pain?
They wake me every night to complain

You screamed in your sleep again
And your words were the same:

Free the wildfowl
Housekeeper!

V

I dreamt I saw a great sea
And a great many people by this sea

So many, so many, like the earth
Emptied its bowels on the shores

And the sea was vast
It stretched and stretched

To the farthest reaches of the sky
Till it merged with the clouds

It was like Bar Beach
Yet it wasn't like Bar Beach

You could see across its waters
As if from Abonema to Yola

And the waters were dark
Like a great mass of pythons

They would heave and swell
And heave and swell

And leap into the air
And fall back again

They would roam this way
And roam that way

Like a huge wounded boa
And settle down again

Then, the sea began to move
Over the shores into the land

Through the forests over the hills
Into the cities into the towns

Swallowing up everything
Trees were falling

Hills were buried
Houses sank into its bowels

Like mammoths in quicksand
And people, people, people

Swam and struggled and drowned
Elders, children, pregnant women

Mothers with children on their backs
Young men and women, big and small

The favored and the poor
A great wailing filled the earth

People struggled and drowned
For, this sea was thick and dark

And afloat were bones and bodies
And stray remains of soldiers' boots

I looked again and saw
And this sea was blood.

VI

I saw them bring in my mother
They were dragging in my mother

And I asked:
Why my mother?

But they forced her to the ground
And I heard the whip crack

I made to start
The ropes held me

A tear quickened from my eye
And spattered on the floor.

VII

Yet, what song is this when
The rhythm is pained?

What pain is this when
The weeping is faint?

My heart goes out like the frail
Hand of a child to its mother

My heart goes out to those who
Must cuddle the earth at Ikpoba

My heart goes out to you
At Gashua, at Kiri-Kiri

Wherever the boots crunch
And swagger sticks pound

And concrete scrapes
The skin from soul

My heart goes out to my own
Kinsmen, my flesh and blood

Who must now be trampled
In this march of bulls

My heart goes out to you irreverent
Rams who must sleep in the rain

Like the hand of a cripple reaching for love
My heart gropes for the face of my mother

My heart goes out to the mothers
The wives, who must bear when

The hawk snatches its game at dawn
My heart goes out to all whose

Sorrow mops the pavements clean
Of the blood of their kin

Those whose tears wet the streets
Those whose souls sorrow weighs

Down like a sack of stones on a mule
Whose tears must now mingle

With mine
A prodigal sings your pain, mothers.

VIII

Love is the stalk that holds the leaf to the tree
Without it the leaf falls and is trampled underfoot

Love is the rope that holds the climber to the trunk
It is love that holds me to you and your own

I love those billion faces
Those sweaty, smiling faces

Those suffering faces
Those trampled faces

Those mudcast images
Of a tortured land

I love them all

I love those young men swarming the cities
From Lagos to Kano like a swarm of locusts

Those black ants crawling on every inch of earth
Covering the streets like a layer of fungi

Flooding the cities like the flood of a broken dam
Flooding into every corner till the quarters are covered

And the alleys are covered and the sidewalks are
Drowned like a landslide seals off the earth

I love the women, backbone and saddle
Tender shoots that pillar the house

Mountain springs that feed the river
Wattle that holds the mud together

Mine is a strained obeisance
I love them all

I love the land
I love the land with its warts and scabs

I love the soil over my umbilical cord
I love the green in the wet season

The living forests thick and fresh
Like the breath of God

The smell of first rain
As it kicks up the dust

I love the taste of the soil

I love the rivers dark and
Rambling like my lines

Those rivers now choking on bodies
And the curse of the Gods

I love the rivers and springs and waterfalls
The sun and the dusk and the crow of the cock

The tongues
The million tongues

One kilometer is another language
But I love them all

Which is more than the love
Of the son for the mother

Or the love of the young man
For his bride or the love

Of the toddler for his maid
Which is the love of the singer for his song

Which is the love of a broken man for life
Which is the tortured cry of love

I love them all

I love the grass
I love the sky

I love the pat on the shoulder
I love the blood in my veins

I love that land
I love

But

Where is your love
Nigeria?

A GATHERING FEAR

for Amaghimonyeodimma and Joshua

And he began to shout for help,
seeing before him the lash,
the fire, and the depthless water,
seeing his head bowed down forever,
he...the lowest among these lowly.

- James Baldwin
Go Tell It on the Mountain

The Voice

They drove him out
Of the neighborhood
And called him names
They pelted him with curses
And jeered at him

But his voice stuck
Like a dagger in their ribs

So, they sought him out
Paraded him in the square
And whipped him raw
Then hounded him
Into the woods

But that voice came
Ringing from the wild

They went after him

And cleared the brambles
And torched the undergrowth
Till they chased him into
The arms of the desert

Yet, when the sun went down
And they retired to sleep
And it seemed as though
Peace might grope its way
Back into their hearts

His voice returned
To haunt their courtyards

Again, they fanned out across
The horizon and combed through
The length and breadth of the desert
And when they found him they
Clobbered him into the sand

And wiped the blood from their hands
And mopped the sweat from their brows
And built a monument over the spot
Where his body lay
And walked away

Then, the voice
Began to howl

That voice sprouted again
And crawled into their skulls
His voice walked ahead
And came from behind and
Rocked their earth to dirt

They did not return
The voice survives.

I am bound to this land by blood

I am bound to this land by blood
That's why my vision is blurred
I am rooted in its soil
And its streams flood my veins
I smell the sweat of its men
And the million feet that plod
The dust of its streets
Leave their prints on my soul
I have walked the footpaths of this land
Climbed the snake-routes of its hills
I have known the heat of its noon
And the fields where men toil till dusk
I have known the faces their creases
I have seen pain engraved on the foreheads
Of many I have heard their agony

I have cried so often with broken men
And peered into a million faces blank
Faces without bodies bodies without faces
The owners of nothing breakers of stone

The owners who are owned
I have known them all

I have heard the wailing of millions
I have stood in the crowd where men
Mixed their sweat and wiped blood
From their brows cursing silently
I have stood in the middle of whirlwinds
And their heat has left its mark
I bear the mark of the masses on my brow

And if I curse
If I raise this single voice
In the midst of dust and curse
If I lend a tiny voice
To the rustle of this crowd
It is because I am bound
To this land

I am bound

To the dying mother the widow
The man with a weight on his loins
I am tethered to their moan they are my own
I belong with they who have no voice
They who trudge outside the gate
They who sigh silently in their hearts
Who only shake their heads

And if I sing not of roses and rivers
It is because I see rivers of blood
I look through the holler of the crowd
And I see blood on the ground
I see blood on the rock slabs
I look across the mangrove swamps
And I walk through the fields of groundnuts
And I see nothing but blood

I see blood in the face of the farmer
On the palm of the school child
I see blood on the statue

Of the Immaculate Mother
I walk through the streets
And I see puddles of blood
I see blood on your shoes on your underwear
I see blood on the hands of men
And if I raise my voice to holler
It is because the grasses wither
In this deluge of blood
Fishes float on their bellies
With their eyes covered
By the sanguine flood

My verse spreads ungathered
In this spill of purple
Mine is the cry of a ram tethered
To the slaughter slab

There are no petals soft
No yellow centers
No polished pebble

Melodies piled into song
My words are rough-hewn from
These rocks where men toil
The plaintive voices of children
The thud of prisoners' feet
The peasant woman's curse
Are the wattle of my song

My pictures are the color of dust
And I sing only of rust
I have swum in the flood
And I know better
For I am bound
To this land
By blood.

Triumphal Entry

I

I see Your Majesty resplendent
Upon the throne of God
The Beast at your feet

I see your gold-sandaled feet
Rest on the spines of men
I hear the creak of their ribs

And the radiance of your laughter
Lights the recesses of heaven
With the blaze of seven suns

I see the hands of the serfs
Whose sweat has robed your feet
In garments of gold

And in the shriveled distance
I hear the howl of dogs
The bay of a hound driven to heat

I hear the sound of a bayonet
Driven through the marrow
Of the womb

The King has not come on the back of a mule
His path paved with branches and leaves
The King has come in the dazzle of butts

Garlands of toilet paper bedeck his neck
The King has come with a split-tooth grin
The King comes riding on the bones of men.

II

Blessed is he that cometh
And blessed, too, the city

Blessed is the land
And its acres of stone

Blessed is the mortar
And the council of war

Blessed is the Virgin
And the Queen of Spades

Blessed is the hand that wrought
The eleventh wonder of the world

Blessed are the meek at heart
Blessed are the poor, the hungry

Blessed are the travelers
Without traveling shoes

III

Bless me, then
And my tongue of steel
The crash of cymbals
And the moan of trombones

Bless the bleeding child
And his broken father
Inheritors of laid-up
Mansions of fiberglass

Bless the fleeing and the fled
Bless the prisoner with his stain
Bless the homecoming of saints

Blessed is the man
With the bloated tongue held
Between the rafters of his feet

Blessed are the poet and his gun
The splinters of his loins
Blessed are his woes.

IV

The moneychangers at the gate
The man with the broken head
The mother of twins
Her wooden dolls
The woman with a hole in her heart

The King blesses them all

The cadavers on the corridors of steel
The tramps on the sidewalk in Oshodi
The hangman the fool
The headmaster of a school
With a welcome address

The King blesses them all

And blessed are we
Who prostrate at his feet
Blessed are we who
Are blessed to see

The scream of sirens
And the gleam of his grin
Blessed is the dust cloud
That rises in his wake
Blessed are the shards
Of his thousand promises

Blessed is he
That cometh in green
Blessed is his name.

Who Would Listen to the Poet?

1

I was traveling through Sagamu
And they stood in my way
I went back, and took the route
Through Abeokuta
I tunneled through darkness
Groping for sunrise
Yet, there they were
Blocking my path

But when I pulled up a palm tree
And used the trunk for chewing stick
They scurried away like harassed fowls
When I mounted Olumo
And began to chew the rocks

They pleaded with me
And bade me farewell

The Bard of Ikere!
Olosunta's child!
Minstrel with a mouth so wide
It cannot be gagged
Crier in the marketplace
Guardian of the word
A true song survives long
After the songbird is gone

I hope my path is clear

Obiora nwa Agulu!
Nwa a muru na nma!
Gifted hand that puts the finishing
Touch where the Gods forgot!
Though ashes mock the returnee
There was beauty here once

I plead for safe passage

I am the bird with the iron tongue
I have sharpened my tongue on a whetstone
My tongue is unsheathed tonight
I want to speak to the King.

2

He raises his hand
And the people prostrate
He brings down his hand
And their cries fill the earth

Kabiyesi!
Guardian of the House
Swaggering chief in a green felt cap
Strong one whose face is mild, like a child's
Yet his heart is as hard as a stonewall
The hyena that laughed his way into the flock
The God's filed his teeth
And blessed them with a slit
But nothing surpasses
The wisdom of the Gods

Your crowd of attendants
Hedge you like a wall
While we watch from afar
Great leader of men!

Who dares defy your cordon of dogs?
Your presence rides ahead of you!

A leader must be tough like a sisal cord
His heart must be hard like a block of iron
Stout one who rocks the foundation of the earth!
Stocky one who defies the cry of all!

Warlord in time of peace!
General with a rusty sword!
Warrior whose shield decorates the bedroom!
We hear of trials and hasty sentences
Of stealth arrests and swift executions
In his bored and idle moments
Even Ogun slaughtered his own

The owl that farts and demands his oriki!
Who dares point a finger in Your Majesty's face?
The tears of broken men quench your thirst
The sight of famished children feeds your pride

Arrogant one with a foul mouth!
He wears little men around his waist
Swashbuckler that chooses noon

To strike down his prey
He awaits his detractors
Behind their own porch
He sets up committees
And overrules them
His emissaries are still on their way
And he arrives ahead of them
He has paved a path of gold
For himself and his own
He has surrounded his homestead
With the shade of money trees

Chameleon with a silent walk!
Ravaging bull that leaves a trail!
The poet salutes you, leader of men!
Let the day untwine the night's entrails

3

We hail you, too, Iyalode!
Aya roro joko lo
Mound of earth that props up the house
Yet speaks louder than the owner of the house

I remember how, once
In a town by the Great River
Men were rounded up like stray roosters
And slaughtered in the open square

Her own father was among them

The poet greets you, Iyalode
She fills the house with foster children
Yet stows hers away to fatten in foreign lands
We hear your children's laughter
Beyond the precincts of the House
And when the heir returns
Flamboyant like his mother
We hear the roar of his motorcycle

From far beyond Epe

Leader of women!
Pride of the weavers' guild!
Peacock whose trunk lacks
No cloth, old or new!
Your scarf is smooth silk
Your buba is rich cotton
On your thin waist adire
Finds itself a perfect home
You adorn your shoulders
With the richest sanya
Fifty lengths of akwete
Sweep the dust behind you
Whoever beholds you beholds
The true wealth of our land

We are a proud people
A people's pride must be seen
In the wealth of their leaders

And especially in the flamboyant
Presence of their First Lady
And the rich scent of her cloth
The glitter of her jewelry
The swagger of her gait

Peacock that strides through
The marketplace with pomp!
Pride of the naked and the half-clad!
She who does not soil her hands
Cooking for a husband
She who does not cook
For a family of ten

Magnanimous leader!
Savior of women!
She neither farms a plot
Nor knows the cost of melon
Whoever has not shaken
The rough hand of the hoe

How can she know the texture
Of our humble lives?

We do not need your charity
Whoever works harder
May they also eat better
The boat that took your children away
May it also have a place for our own
That the eagle may perch
That the kite, too, may perch

That is all we ask
Great Mother of the Nation
Queen of the famished
Mother who fills her kitchen
With the din of a hundred children
Yet steals her own children away
To fatten in foreign lands.

4

There is hunger in the land
Cries of anguish fill the House
A storm gathers on the outskirts
Yet, how would dogs set on a death path
Be able to tell the smell of excreta?

The King and His court have gone to feast
While the howls of the starving rise in the square
Who can keep a drunk fly from drowning?

Oya warned Ogun
In his moment of folly
But, your women, too, are drunk
Their leaden ears blocked by
The chink of wine glasses and
The chatter of their jewels

The warlords are blinded
By the dazzle of power
For, who dares defy

The radiance of the King?
Who dares raise a finger
Against the court of giants?

Yet, once, in a land by the Great River
There was a giant named Anukili
With the crook of one hand
He could throw seven men
Wherever he set foot
He left craters in the earth
Slouching beast that shook the forest
With the strength of ten lions
Terror of villages far and wide
What man could stand up
To the great scourge of warriors?

Anukili was drunk on the strength of his arms
Anukili harvested where he had not sown
He ravished farmlands

And stripped yam barns
He took men's wives
And took their land, too
Where Anukili reaped corn
He sowed scorn in its place
Wherever he walked
Pain and anguish marked his trail
The cries of famished children fed his pride

When one man cooks for a party of many
They quickly clear his broth, but, when a party
Of many cooks for one man...

Anukili's people met and threw a challenge
Whoever could heave a thatch roof
All the way to the river
That man would be King
That man would rule forever

And who, but Anukili
Could face down such challenge?

The fool builds his house on mud
Believing there's nothing else to life
But the strength of his arm

With the stoutest ropes he could find
Anukili bound a thatch roof to his frame
And set out for the river
The people lined the forest path
And bathed his name in praises:

> *Anukili the Great*
> *Pride of all men*
> *Terror of warriors*
> *Who would reign over us*

Midway to the river

They set fire to the roof

What one man can down the communal broth?
Which power can defy the wisdom of all?

A people is like a bunch of oil palm fruits
No man can bear it in one palm
And he who stirs and stirs
And stirs a cub awake from slumber
Must stand and face the whirlwind
When the sleeping cub awakes.

5

He raises his hand
And the people prostrate
He brings down his hand
And their cries fill the earth

Kabiyesi!
Guardian of the House
The one whose heavy title
Cannons through the land
Your men hedge you like a stonewall
Fear and terror clear your path
Yet the Okra does not outgrow
The owner of the garden
No one can clear the broth of all
No power long survives
The wrath of the wronged

The seer howls his fears
Into the open air, yet, who
Among these cavaliers would listen?

A Gathering Fear

I

The demented set his hut on fire
And stood aside to watch the ashes of his life
The child is set again on a path of death
And my fear returns to me

The seven-feathered whydah
Foul-mouthed emissary whose cries doom the earth
The whydah cries itself hoarse in the precincts
And this fear returns to me

The flesh-eating bird has appeared
On the travelers tree, and vultures in their
Committees promenade the square
I have known these seasons

I have known this harshness
Threatening the very breath of earth
These clouds now hurrying back
Heralding the clap of thunder

We've walked this path before
Memory lies ahead wreathing in her pain
The nightmare has just begun
And my fear returns to me

Whoever recalls the rampaging bull
Rumbling tanks crunching bone in dust
Bristling youth eternally ground into mud
The exile train with its burden of shame

The widowed mother and her shriveled child
Whoever recalls those desolate scapes
Whoever recalls the scent
Of his own brother's blood

Let him watch these seasons
Let him tread softly
Into this dance
Of masquerades.

II

Across the city
In the quarter of the noble
And outside in the fair grounds
Behind the stonewalls

Praise-singers and madmen
Test the hide of their drums
The rich have brought out wine
Flung their iron gates ajar
The guests are gathered with their guards
And their women garbed in gold

They make merry in the grounds
Bata drumming and fire flares
They make merry while the land
Creaks and groans under their feet

The streets are cleared of the blind
The slums and tramp quarters bulldozed
The sidewalks are festooned

With cloth banners and lights

The cries of the humble
Are drowned in the drumming
The grime along the alleys
Freshly whitewashed and primed
Tonight, for once
This city shall be free

Yet, somewhere in the distance
A lame dog is dripping blood
Up the street of beggars
Through the dark alleys

Beyond the stonewalls
Past the gates where
Prisoners rehearse their death
Into the quarter of the noble
And there, cries of anguish
Mingle with the drumming

The skyline is grey now
And at dawn there will be no sound
For this city will be found
Drowned in its own blood.

III

What do mourners search for
In a cobblestone square?

These widows have come
To the wrong place

There are no bones inside the tomb
Of the Unknown Citizen

His murderers keep the bones
Each day cleaners scrub

The palace clean of bloodstains
And orphans search in vain

There is only sorrow
For the widow here

In a land of mad men
There's only anguish and pain

While silence paves the road
To the commoner's grave.

IV

The fool has rolled out his gown
And taken to the streets
Oh! How short memory!

The fool has taken to the streets
And in the heat of the afternoon
His voice rings in the marketplace
Above the stench of his sores
The fool ignores his own footprints
Still wet with blood

In the city there is fear
In the alleys sprout seeds of terror
Yet the horsemen gallop on

At night
In hidden places
Robbers prowl
With their masks down
They ignore the dog
Howling at the moon.

V

Generals
Sergeants
Warlords
Who feed on blood

Carrion eaters
Pallbearers
Tin gods who reap
Where they did not sow

Your shrines are empty

Patriarchs of crumbling quarters
Presidents for life
Founding fathers who founded
Only their own estates

Your shrines are empty

The rich ones howl in the lanes

Proclaiming their wealth
But your house is built of ashes
Your shrines are empty

You have built your barn of riches
In the path of a storm
You have sown your seeds
Among the dry grass

Now the aged and the bled
Have taken to the streets
And dead children curl up
In the fields like dry leaves

And you have slain
Many more with hunger
Than you have slain
With the sword

The sun is astir with rage

The sea froths in its mouth
And soon the earth will crumble
Like a shell under your feet

Your shrines are empty.

VI

Who can save the Land in this evil hour?
What force can hold down the flood
And the inexorable earthquake?

The only way forward
From here is backward
The only route to tomorrow
The only path home
For the wandering child
Is backward

The only way beyond this chasm
Yawning with the mischief
Of a monumental fall
This rapid-whirling whirlpool
Hungry with the hunger of a lion
The only way forward from here
Is backward

Ah! But Death knocks on the door of this nation

Death struts outside the city gates
And there is no escape
Death has appeared on horseback
Ahead of his ravaging cavalry
And the city walls are crumbling
The barricades are tumbling
The men have gone in with their wives
The guards have sheathed their knives

Death has seized this nation in his grip
And there is no escape

I see the ashes of a great city
I see the ruins of a great lie
I see the tongues of fire ravish
The city and its children

And all the cattle
And all the sheep
And all that breathe

Within the city

All the high-rises are down
All the monuments of shame
And the birds lie wounded

In the streets

I see the flames of wrath thunder
And there is naught to describe it

Yes, there is no way forward
But through the Blood River.

VII

The puddle in the shard sits for the poodle
So, let the spear split the granite
Lightning bears the torch for thunder
So, let the spear shatter the rock

I seek refuge here, Yemisi
Now that the clouds threaten
And the scent of storm rides the dust
And Peace lies exhausted

On the ground

Lead me out in the grass
Lay me close to the earth
This earth of my beginning
The earth owns us all

We are mere children
Scrubbing our bellies
Innocence clothed in grime
Memory is stale breath

Now that the horsemen have returned
With their swords glinting in the sun
And the Beast charges unleashed
At our plot of dreams

Roll the beads
Unfold the mat of your bosom
Shield this child of a bondswoman
Let your tears squelch

The raging fever within
And when tonight the earth shudders
Hauling corpses from unmarked graves
Spread your arms, daughter

Hide this chick shivering
From the fleet of kites hovering
Holding the square under
The curse of their breath.

Lament for the Changeling

for Dambudzo Marechera

When he died
They laid him out
Wrapped in plantain leaves
Before the Stone Bird

There they unwrapped him
His face gleaming with sweat
Like he was only asleep
No one could believe it

Ogbanje!
Trespasser in the land of men
Streak of lightning before rain
Before you shudder, he is gone

Stray riff of a distant flute
Sailing on windwing
Destined for other lands
Brief as an eyelid bat

The rainbow, they say
Does not last till dusk
A pallbearer does not
Wait around for kolanuts

Omenuko!
Migrant minstrel
In a season of drought
Vagrant with a rattle tongue

He carried his skinbag
Of tales in one hand
While in the other he held
A fistful of stones

Despised at home among his own
Feared abroad, wherever he trod
They robed him in a sash of fame
And put a shackle on his name

Yet, who could chain a weaverbird?
Who could snare a gust of wind?
Vapor spirit of the night
He shamed both manacle and leash

Agwuishi!
He will walk these paths again
Fleeting spirit of Wahungwe!
What rare beauty to commit to earth!

Lament for the Gazelle

for Thomas Sankara

The gazelle's terrain is the grassland
The lion is king in the wild

The eagle perches on the Iroko
The eagle is king among birds

I pray to our ancestors for light

Death appears before a monarch
And he falls on his knees and pleads

Death calls on the arrogant
And he prostrates in the dust

Death that snatches the eagle

And leaves the vulture unscathed

Death has snatched the fury from the whirlwind
Death has snatched away the leopard of Burkina

Ah! Master of men!

Master who strikes down a youth
When life is sweetest to him

Master who strikes down the sapling
Yet spares the ancient mangrove

Death has struck down
The masquerade in the square

I pray to our ancestors for light

The times are cloudy and
The footpath is wet

If the blind loses his stick
The future becomes a wall

Evil walks abroad wielding a club
Cowards stomp in the dusty arena

Fools dig up ancient hooves
And urinate on graves

Sorcerers swing our fate
From jeweled little fingers

Night has unleashed hyenas
And wolves upon the land

Death has taken the goatherd
So rustlers may run wild

Let's pray to our ancestors for light.

The youth who dances

The youth who dances
Only when his mother sings
When his mother dies
His dance will cease

What song shall I sing
In a strangers' market square?

At home they turned me out and said:

> *This is no time for dirges*
> *Here is no place for laments*
> *What we need are praise-singers*
> *We need cheerleaders*

And I turned to them and asked:

> *Can't you see that the hut is on fire?*
> *Can't you smell the coming of the locust plague?*

But they jeered one and all and said:

This is only the night of bonfires
We need dancers around the blaze
Acrobats and drummers, stilt dancers
And, listen carefully, lest you forget

The toddler who makes haste
To find what killed his father
Had better beware, else what took
His father might claim him, too

Bitterness only ruins the song
We need laureates!
Weavers of words!
We want dancers!

A gun is a mere stick
If the gunpowder is wet

What pride has the thatch-maker
If his mother's roof leaks?

The prophet's voice has faded
With the jangle of his manacles
What more is there to say?
What song now remains?

Summer Song

I will walk the streets today
And ride the crest of the sun
Gather the glitter of summer
The blinding textile of flowers

Sip the yellows and the reds
Like nectar or sparkling wine
Drown in the riotous carnival
Of colors and scented flesh

I will ride atop the double-decker
Bus and drink merrily of the wind
With the dark skin of the tarmac
Stretching underneath me

Past the busy cash points
And their long, restless queues
Lovers holding hands
Lovers holding down their lust

Yes, I will leave behind
The crushed daisies from home
The General's grinning face
And the roll call of the jailed

The images of mothers with photos
Of their missing and their dead
I will leave them all behind today
And drift with the train of tourists

I will take a walk through the galleries
Watch matinees at Oxford Circle
Heckle orators with the crowds at Hyde Park
Embrace the world with laughter

Then, I will sit alone in the open
Among the naked sunbathers
And wrestle with my lines
And the graveyards inside

And the young women shall walk
Up to me, ignore their impatient lovers
And leaning in on my raging heart
Gently say to me:

You are a poet or something

And I will answer and say:

Yes, a poet of wounds
I am a man of constant sorrow
Driven from his homeland
And severed from his kind
A blade of palm frond floating

And they shall open my breast
And find within: the barb, the flag
A map of my country
And a boiling sea of tears.

Poem for a Soldier

In memory of M. Vatsa

A chubby soldier with a scarified face
His lips were dry like Harmattan
Dark as the barrel of a gun

He wrote poetry and sang for children
Took photos of flowers and rare birds
He loved the smell of the great outdoors

And reveled in the rocks and sunshine
In his soul rivers ran in lyrical lines
Like the blood that he trained to shed

He was no saint; his hands were stained
For what soldier but the cowardly

Is entirely free of the stench of blood?

But he loved to sing and gave to the arts
He carried his camera like a shotgun
And where others wore holstered steel

He carried a pouch of graphite and lead
He preferred the reading desk to the trench
And communed with writers rather than drunks

Dark was the day when they picked him out
And hung a coup d'état around his neck
They paraded him naked through the streets

And hurried him through the dock
Back in the barracks, they
Gambled for his clothes

With his poems they fed campfires
And broke his pencils one by one

O, how he sat shackled among the hyenas

Stripped and cold, surrounded by hate
Wise men pleaded on his behalf
Working men washed their hands of his blood

But the sword cannot follow the logic of a poem
Or pigs discern the scent of sunflowers
While the nation waited for news of his fate

And philosophers pondered the nature of his plight
His jailers knocked on the door of his cell
And dragged him out in the dark of night

They led him to the edge of the sea
And pinning his body down on the shore
They tore out his fingers one by one

The right hand first, and then the left
The fingers that held both pen and gun

One by one they flung them into the sea

Then, they tore his hands from his shoulder
Blades; the right hand first, and then the left
They burnt his toenails and ate his eyes

Then clawed out his heart and quartered it
And raising each piece to the candlelight
They searched for residues of his verse

What little they saw, they scraped with their
Swords; an unfinished poem about crocodiles
A little ditty for his youngest daughter

His books they poured into an armor trunk
And tying the trunk to his savaged remains

Lowered his body into the sea

They gave us the news on television
With faces drawn by the burden of death
Layers of make-up could barely conceal

The fresh blood dripping from their lips
We fed his body to the dogs, they said
The law is no respecter of persons

We fed his flesh to the fowls of the air
The sword is no respecter
Of pens.

The Emperor and the Poet

for J. Mapanje

when the dogs
took Jack away
they thought they
would find peace

if only they could
kill them all
poets & artists
the pitiful lot

hang them all
and burn their books
or make them write
with their own blood

feed them dung
then crack their skulls
just wipe them out
like weeds or bugs

but then, from jail
Jack sent them word
he'd call their bluff
and damn their gods
he'd walk and talk
and not once stop
till he'd see them fall
and watch them crawl

until then
each poem and song
would be a noose around
the emperor's neck.

Sketch for a Eulogy

They wrote me from home saying:

The pumpkins are dying
The cocoyams are dry
The earth has turned
Into a bowl of dust

I have come to see
The mother of the dead
So, let the crying cease
Let the teeth-gnashing end

When I told the council

That I saw dead pigeons in my dream
The elders merely shifted in their seats
The learned with their books
Only saw letters in black

The rivers and streams flooded that year

There was blood in their stool
Bones sprouted on the seashores
Where the rich swam in their pools

News came from Lagos

They had slaughtered an only son
And fed his flesh to the Emperor's dogs
Soldiers prowled the streets at dawn
Thrusting bayonets through each door

I have come to see the slain
That I may put a finger in his wound
Blood of my blood Blood of my Land
That I may plant a palm tree in His breast.

Letter to His Mother

it's raining again today
it always rains
but the blood in the streets
is dry and brown
may be it'll loosen now
there are men out on the street
covered in bin lining
shoveling blood into barrows
all day. all night.
under the endless rain
more blood running
in the open
drains.

*

something's eating at my soul.
an insect nibbles at the edges
slowly, slowly, scraping away
corroding waters lapping up
the underbelly of the sea.
my soul is a clump of Black
earth sitting on water, but
how long can it last? how long
can the donkey bear its load?
slowly, the inside crumbles
piece by piece
grain after grain
floating away on the
dark, green sea
sinking
with
time.

*

do i remember my name?
i remember my name.
a word in two syllables.
silent as a stab.
and my country
i remember
        faces
and
        snatches
of what once was.
memory stammers.
nothing remains
but a two-inch scar.
i hang my life on the wall
like a crushed jacket,
across the gulf
a tightrope arcs and sways,
thin as a strand of hair.
inside, a cauldron roars
with boiling oil shooting
white steam into my skull.

*

i carry your pictures still
but what is there in pictures?
the mind is the only picture.
the mind is a crumpled photograph
fraying at the edges
fading, aging
slowly gathering dust.
the gag is still in place
and my stitches bleed.
the face in the mirror
is a ghost only the
mirror changes with
terror in its eyes
its back to the wall.

*

when the last vein snaps
please scatter my ashes
in the quarter of the poor
down in the crumbling alleys
where the dogs lie
i walk in circles now
uttering the last word
mantra. sutra
petri. patra
sultry word
sultry world
speech is dead.
any minute now
the dome will give
and crush the soul.
there'll be no blood.
the lamp still burns.
the lamp will burn
till the wicker
in the marrow

runs its course
and then
darkness.

Song for Nigeria

I

I sing of you today,
Land of my beginning
Today when the world is still
And a trillion eyes are turned on you
As you do your wobbly dance
And your children scratch their brows
While the earth roars in laughter
I sing of you
Land of my beginning

I sing of you, Nigeria
From these shores I sing your name
    for I am you
    as you are me

and you are the mother
as I am the child
and nothing can stand
between the offspring
and the womb

I sing of you
land of a million suns
land of forests and of hills
land of the rich land of the poor
land of high-rises and tramps

I sing of you, Homeland
the head that once stood high
the feet that once pounded the earth
and it shook and shuddered
the eyes that once could shame the sun
are now covered in shame

I sing of you

land of money is no object
land of obituaries and naming ceremonies
land of public holidays
land of anniversaries

I sing of you
land of laze man na im poor
land of craze man fit be president
don't mind the bloody civilians
who im pear ripe, make e lick

I sing your workers
the coal diggers, tin miners
tillers of the soil -
monkey de work, baboon de chop -
without them where would we go?
the shoe makers, the blacksmiths
road transport workers
rail transport workers
the office workers in

dainty sleeve shirts
toiling on files day after day
living on bank overdrafts
Onitsha market traders association -
it's great wealth makes Onitsha swagger
- Ariara timber traders association
the street traders and truck-pushers
the bus drivers, taxi drivers
the truck drivers who, like a husband,
can tell your contours in the dark
the oil drillers and rig workers
struggling and dying
on the vast, cruel seas
filling each barrel
with their very blood
those barrels of oil
you hand to the world
on which your tyrants feed

I sing your cities, too

coalcity, gardencity, ivorycity
city of the river of crocodiles
dirt is only on the skin
it does not hide beauty

I sing your singers, your minstrels
the ones who dirge with a smile
the true owners of the voice

I sing of you
land of wealth and waste
land of shards and ruins
the bitch and her iron leash
one nation bound in freedom, peace and unity

my pride
my shame
my love
my curse
I sing your name today

but my song is sparse and coarse
and it's bitter on my tongue.

II

Don't drive me mad, Nigeria
Don't twist me, bend me, break me
Like you've broken those eighty million youths
Now dragging their bodies through your streets
Each one a portrait of anguish

Don't drive me too hard, I am delicate like a child
Don't club me with memories or break my limbs
Don't kick me in the head
Don't butt me with your gun
Don't drive your wedges between my joints
I am young, Iam
An innocent man

Don't threaten me further
Let your hyenas, vultures, emperors, chiefs
Your governors, generals, gunslingers, thieves
Those murderers and pimps who run your affairs
Keep their hands off me
I am a child of the war

I have bitterness in my blood

Don't give me any
Of your smile, either
Or pat me on the head
I need to pay my rent, your levies, your taxes
I need to pay school fees
hospital bills
water rates
sanitation fees
license for my transistor radio
license for my bicycle
bribes to the nurse
bribes to the tax officer
bribes to the official
selling fertilizers
bribes to the policeman
so I can move about freely
so I can walk in the open
and breathe fresh air

I need kerosene and firewood
I have children to feed
I need a job, dear Fatherland
I am strong of mind and bone
I want to earn my bread
I need a roof over my head

It is too cold tonight I am freezing under the bridge I am huddled in a bundle in this colony of tramps with no blanket on my back I might even die before dawn I am one of your "leaders of tomorrow" I have no home to go to there is no future on this road I don't even want to die I am a sore on your face!

There is no metaphor to capture
The agony of the rest

And don't you put me in jail
Like you have so many others
It won't clear up this mess

Or build more houses
Or pay the teachers
Or stop the coups
Or keep America from
Breathing down your neck
You brought in ant-infested logs
You must play host to lizards

If you have me butchered
And hauled over Eko Bridge
Would that clear the mystery
Of the murdered journalist?

Would it wipe out beggars
Or stop student riots?
Would you kill all the blind?
Would you kill hunger with a stick?
There's a fire raging in the house
And you're chasing after rats
You turn away from the broad path

And you wade through elephant grass
You've shed so much blood already
Your fingers are soiled with blood
You dance out of step
Your dance is a dance of death

Can you hear me, Nigeria
Am I knocking on a wall?

It's not me that you're looking for
I am only a poet.

III

After the mortuaries are emptied of their latest guests
After the mass graves are dug
After the midnight burials, the hidden funerals
After the soldiers have returned
With their spades and washed their feet
After the landscaping and silences
Tell me, Homeland
Can we cover up the sky?

Children tucked into bed at night by their fathers
Wake up and never see them again
Wives wait for their husbands
Fathers for their sons
And they never return
Across your breadth
Households ache and moan
Families clutter to mourn
Young men frothing with life
Like fresh palm wine
Their hands clean and

Their minds pure as
The morning after rain
Are brought down in the street
In a smear of blood and brain
Yet thieves walk around in
Uniform slapping their thighs
Obscenities fill the TV screen
And call me "fellow countrymen"
Tell me: Did we fight off the fox
So we can slaughter the chicks?

Grief traces a path
No bulldozer can tear
Anger is a pregnancy
You cannot cup it with the palm
I have seen men wrench back tears
With fists crashed into the wall
You're only picking your way
Through a path of patient mines
The child who shakes his head

Today and gnashes his teeth
Is counting his years
Someday he will answer
With a flaming sword
The fowl that steps back
To crush its own eggs
Who will mourn it
When the big stick strikes?

I sing you
As I sing myself
The child dreads
The depths of night
I have aged in my youth
Wrinkled with rage
Fury fills every inch
Of my flesh with broken glass
My shoulders sag and bow
Like a withering seedling
I have worn my soul with worry

And I shiver in my bones
I look at you
And I say to myself

Is this all there is?
A field of tragedies?
Acres of stone?
In this hour of grief
Can we turn
Even to the young?

You are a burden, Nigeria
You are a crown of thorns.

IV

Odo has taken
The highway to Lagos
The wild one has taken
The four o'clock bus
He took nothing with him
Only his head and his sack of verse
He left nothing behind
But the ashes and dry grass
Wayward minstrel!
Blind bull on a crowded street
Brushfire that blazes
In the afternoon sun
Blunt machete on shin
Wherever you go
May your path be clear!
Your lines are deep and
Furious, like a mountain river
Dark, fierce,
A path of acid
Knife wounds

In the belly of the earth
Your howl scours the heart
Like a hoe on dry earth
Yet, your songs are beautiful
Like a woman, slim, fine boned
Skin of kernel balm

I sing your name
That I, too, may be sung
I sing your name, Odo
That your voice may thunder
At my funeral
That your anger
Like your voice
May rip the sun
From the sky
And like a whip-
Wielding masquerade
Scatter the dogs
From the graveside

I want to be buried at noon

And you, Iké
Wiry one with the
Temper of a log fire
Whatever took speech from you
Gave the pen in return
If dreams are mere mud
Resolves are the wattle
That hold it together
The penis has no bone
It is the will that makes it stand
We sat together on footpaths
And mourned the Fatherland
Hauled stones, wiped
Our tears on the flag
I was with you then and
The soil was under our feet
Now, here I am
A sojourner in strange lands

Dirgeing still
For, what can a poet do?

Every exile is a hornbill
The Homeland is buried
In his head
She is to him
Like the tortoise's carapace
A hole for retreat
A house of dreams
I have wrapped my dreams
Around that Land
I drag her with me
Like a snail its shell
Emperors come and
One day they go
Tyrants and giants
They all have but one life
Whoever climbs a palm tree on his back
Eventually comes down on his back

All metal end up at the smithy
Nothing outlives the sea

I'm keeping the faith
For that is my breath
Without enduring faith
I am naked and dead
And if my years be blown
Away in distant lands
Like husks of millet
In Harmattan wind
I want to be buried
In a free country
Among my own people
Beside my ancestors

I want no accolades
No eulogies by the grave
No headstone, no epitaph
I ask that no tears be shed

Keep the moist-hearted away
All maize wither after harvest

However, in death
Let my burden be light
Let my heart be free
From this sorrow, this torture
This agony, this pain
This shame that pegs me down
And ropes me like a lamb
And stands me out in the crowd
Like a man covered in dung
Let the soil that covers
My bones be moist with rain
Trodden by the feet
Of all that I have loved
And as I trail the echoes of the valley
Of the shadow of death
Among you let it be said:

There was beauty
In his heart
And the Homeland
Was his song.

SONGS FOR CATALINA

for Catalina Ferrera

1

Catalina mia muy amada

When I looked into your eyes
On that Guadalajara night
I knew that I was staring
Into the depths of the sea

I was born on the highlands
But I always loved the sea
When I looked into those eyes
My whole body shook with thirst

Your face shone around them
Like a freshly washed beach
Free of the feet of tourists
With their unnamable sins

Your dark lips were the edges
Where the waters kiss the shores
Teasing and taunting

In an endless mating brawl

Your nose was the hill
Behind which the sun retires
Smiling as her lover
Burns to ashes with desire

Beloved Catalina
Your eyes were like the sea
Upon which my yearning crashes
With the impatience of waves.

2

You walk with the lightness of a guava leaf
As it dances its way through the evening breeze
You walk with the ease of a silent sun
Flirting its way into the arms of dusk

You walk like a mating dance, my love
Like the shimmer of a pool caressed by light
And the air that you part without a rustle
Knocks me flat like a jug of tequila

Your walk is the flutter of a butterfly
The silent stroll of pollen across the fields
The metronome of your leisured steps
Seduces like the lyrics of a serenade.

3

Poeta laureado vagabundo
I gave up my youth so I could mourn my country

Love I have known, but sorrow is my name
Dying, it seems, is the passion of poets

Moments when I lost the will to proceed
Convinced the only way to go was down

I looked to my country for a ray of light
Found nothing but the charred remains of laughter

Along the streets sparrows die in their droves
Children are born with nooses around their necks

How often I have prayed for the courage to die
In the market of misery, even death is hard to find

Only love has fuelled the wicker in my heart
The love that I found in your fathomless eyes.

4

I will serenade my Beauty
On the streets of Monterrey
In the fading light of evening
When the larks have gone to sea

I will serenade my little one
With the music that she loves
With the luscious beetroot rhythm
Of a Liverpudlian band

I will celebrate our love
With a thousand lines of verse
Do my dance through Nuevo León
With her sweet name on my lips

When the meadowlarks return
They will find me in her lap
As I drown my life's regrets
In the fragrance of her hair

I will whistle heady tunes
Down the valley of her breasts
And with kisses write my name
All over her little feet.

5

Shall I write you sonnets
        with pentametric lines
Rhyming each word
        with the one before?

Shall I do a hip-hop
        routine on the floor
And bring the whole house
        down in your name?

Shall I drag out a tune
        on the violin
Or do a flamenco
        on a box guitar ?

Shall I call your name
        in my mother tongue
Garnished with a flourish
        of talking drums?

Perhaps, I'll do a serenade
	on a bamboo flute
Seduce your spirit
	with a thumb piano tune.

Shall I lead you out
	through the corridors of night
And whistle without sound
	into your inner ear?

May be you'd prefer
	a midnight rave
With five thousand watts
	of acid house

How shall I sing my delight
	mi amora?
How shall I word the warmth
	on my tongue?

6

You remind me of my first love
You, precious little thing
You send fervor surging through my veins
Like sap through bamboo stems

The lush green of your pubescence
Reminds me of home
Of the lusty dance of April corn
After early morning rain

Like a withered seedling touched
By the soothing tongue of rain
My soul begins to heave again

And like a cool touch of humus
Your youth entices my roots
Into depths as yet unknown.

7

For those who weep daily in their sleep
For those who attend to pyres
For those who stand at the gates of sorrow
For undertakers of dreams

For poets whose nibs are poisoned
By the thickening blood of martyrs
Love even in its minutest measure
Is a treasured visitation

Today a fire ravages my soul
With the conflagration of oilfields
And there are here the ecstasies
And there are here the wounds

There are here the flaky smiles
The face aways, the deafened ears
The hourly struggle to forget
The soldiers on the streets

And I slip again
Into the habit of pain
But how does one forget
Friends jailed and dead

Schoolboys shot in the head
The grief on my country's face?
There are here the agony and shame
There are here a poet's rivulets of tears

There are, Catalina, in this epistle of passion
Slivers of a shredded heart
And your love even in its minutest measure
Is a treasured visitation.

8

Encanta mia
My runaway desire
I will sing your name from dawn
Nor rest my tongue till sundown

Elemental waterfall
As close to touch as the horizon
I will drench my soul in your vapour spray
Till I tingle in the marrow

In Buenos Aires they assemble
The dry bones of the missing
Cheap trinkets, plastic wristwatches
A copper tooth here and there

Beside the mothers' testimonies
The photographs and the tears
They build the final monuments
To the Decade of the Beasts

But here, Catalina mia
When the summer rains subside
I plant your face among the rosebushes
And print your name on my guitar.

9

Under a Coca-Cola billboard
On Avenida Pablo Neruda
They sat me down and asked me
What happiness is

Happiness, I said
Is a child from Monterrey
A quetzal whose misty eyes
Are like the sweetness of tears

And down in Tlaquepaque
In the Hall of Refugees
A minstrel moaned a tune
Wondering what happiness is

Happiness, I said
Is a song from Monterrey
Its lines clean and serene
As the notes of a new guitar

Santa Catalina
Scent of cinnamon flowers
Inflorescence of lemons
Over the plains of Nuevo León

Happiness, I say
Is to stare into your face
And feel your innocent gaze
Caress the strings of my soul.

10

The moon mourns her love tonight
But my soul is satisfied

And though the sea unfurls her shroud
Heavy as a stone with tears

And maidens dry their reddened eyes
In the back alleys of town

There's a carnival in my blood
Where the sky touches the earth

The crickets whip their orchestra
Of flutes and tambourines

And the night, like a wall painting
Drips orange over blue

In the fireplace embers burn
Like the red lips of the sun

And flames gyrate with the frenzy
Of drunks on a bridal night

This night is our night, amora
Wherever in the world you are

You virgin apparition dissolves
Distance's wall of pain

And the moon may mourn her loss
My soul is satisfied.

feb 16 '08
Rockefeller

It was autumn
And the air was crisp & fresh
And ~~rejuvenating for the soul~~
the ~~sun~~ early morning sun ~~was bright &~~
~~was~~ bright & innocent
was rejuvenating for the soul
We sat, in the park by a fountain
alone
It was quiet
But for the syncopated laughter
of the water
I loved you then
And I adore you still
Your ~~eyes~~ face eyes were radiant and the dizzle of the
fountain spray reflected your smile, I remember you
now

Radiant & Content, like a Cherry in bloom

Your face was flushed

It was autumn
And the air was crisp & fresh *
clean
The early morning sun
Bright and innocent
Was rejuvenating for the soul
We sat alone
By a fountain in the park
~~It was quiet~~
And But for the syncopated laughter
of the water, all was quiet
Your face was flushed
And your eyes were radiant
And the dizzle of the fountain spray
Reflected your smile / I remember you ~~now~~.

there was delight in your eyes & the dizzle

LATER VERSE

Like a wanderer lost
in the hollowness of words.

Song of Sorrow

for rosa diez

Si podien, però, durar
la llum parada

I shall sing you a song of sorrow
When the moment comes
It is the way of poets
He will come bearing along his voice
Like the lament of an old guitar
Only, night shall fall, another day dawn
I shall sing you a tearful song

In the desert, the rain fell on me
Brushfires danced their way through
The undergrowth of my verse
Your footfall soft as felt, you
Stepped into the light and

Asked the poet for a song
I shall sing you a lyric of pain.

The blue moon peers through the bough
Of your eyelashes; the minstrel hawks
His tears through the streets of night
A household god is asking for water
An old god is pleading at your door
There's a white rose on your breast
It is the fortune of poets
I shall sing you a song.

Untie the fresh leaves of dawn
I want to make my journey short
I shall go up on the hill and cast my little net
Decorate the river of your morning with petals
I shall speak the words of songs
It is the destiny of poets
I shall sing you a song of sorrow
When the moment comes.

Alone

for an unnamed love

Without you, Guru,
Three and three make five;
When I switch on the lights,
Everything goes dark.

Alone with you,
I am in my element.
I strut and chatter
Like a weaverbird.

Words come to me
Like showers of rain,
And my soul convulses
With the power of song.

Alone without you,
I drift in the shadows
Like a bird wounded in flight.

Grief consumes my soul
Like a long winter's night,
And I can hardly sing in the dark.

Gypsy Ballad

Gipsy ballad
Savage night
Bosa nova
Mocking bird

Broken lyre
Sea of tears
Melancholia
Leaf of myrrh

My love, my love
You are the apostrophe
In my song

The fields are aflame with sunflowers
The skies abuzz with weaverbirds

And my yearning runs wild
Like a ravaging flood

My Love
My command
Fugitive word
Lonely dawn

Willowy skies
The whistle of pines
Hour of departure
Blade of grass

Mine, mine
You are the ellipse in my verse
You are the silence in my tears.

A Night at the Coliseum

for Alice

In the womb of the Coliseum
Where emperors and serfs
Once bathed in blood,

I sat at your feet with
My head in your lap,
Under a shower of songs.

The night was dark and shivery.
The niches were lit in blue.
There was dew in your hair.

Silk shawl across your bare
Shoulders, you sat, iridescent
Like a dove, fragile in the dark;

While seven children clad in white
Bore olive branches across a bridge,
To the plaintive tune of violins

And the jangle of tambourines.

They laid the branches at your feet,
And sang your name into the wind,
And you floated gently into the night,

Like a leaf on a country creek.
I reached for you, but you were gone.
I bore the wound of your departure.

All night I sat and thought of you,
Imagined you still next to me, your breath
On my breath, your breast on my breast,

Alabaster on marble: resting.

Right through till dawn I repeated your name.
I felt your face, caressed your lips,
Imagined the taste of your tongue

On my tongue: I suffered.

O, how my errant soul pleaded in vain
At your door like a gladiator with his Queen!
Now I clutch your relic

Like a fragment of a dream.

For the Martyrs of Kurdistan

I came to sing an elegy
And to speak of sorrow and death

But the more I think of you, my friends
The more I think instead of flowers

I, too, come from a stony place
Born as I was in a nation of graves

Where children plead for bread
Yet receive lead in their plates

I, too, come from the very depths
Of the valley of the shadow of death

Where weaverbirds die in the streets
Where grenades are detonated in

The bodies of the innocent
And the wicked sow their mines

Along the boulevards of love
To you, then, my good friends

Who died that your children may live
And that birds may sing again in your

Dawn and pigeons gather in your
Squares to feed from the hands of saints

To you who stood in the path of tanks
Bullets tracing halos over your heads

To you who waved the flag of your land
In the face of bombs and shellfire

To you who stared murderers in the face and said
'Freedom or death; we shall never bow!'

To you who held your fists high in the air
And took the bullets in your chests

Standing straight on your feet, refusing
To renounce the blood in your veins

To you who sang to your last breath
Filling the footpaths of your dis

Membered land with the poetry of your
Bravery and the music of your blood

To you who played the tenbur with your pen
And fought with words instead of guns

To you, and you, to all of you
Man, woman and suckling child

Sisters and mothers
Brothers and martyrs

Pillars of fire
Shields of steel

To you I offer my nib and pen
To you a toast of the living tongue

To you the index finger resting delicate
On the trigger like a lover's breath

To you the voice, the eyes, the
Long-suffering knee

To you the aching heart
The scent of sacrifice

A mother's warm embrace
The lover's silent cry

To you, Musa Anter, Halit
Gungen, Hafiz Akdemir

To you, Burhan Karadeniz
O, Warm blood of youth!

To you, Kemal Kiliç
To you, Yahya Ohran

To you whom I never knew yet
Came to know like I know my own

To you who still sleep and fight
Up in the hills in the winter chill

To you whom I have named
To you whom I have not

I came to sing an elegy
To speak of sorrow and death

Instead, tonight, I sing your memory
Your courage and your sacrifice

I sing the flag and country
That rise in your wake.

Winter approaches like a cancerous death

for Sudeep Sen

That I, too, could spend my days like the nightingale,
with continents and seasons under my wings.

Winter approaches like a cancerous death,
Excruciating, yet certain as Fate,
This merciless coding of exile years.

Again where, once, Hope, cowering, lurked,
Shivering in his second-hand autumn coat,
Little remains but the drunken hurt.

Year after year, the distance grows
Between the exile and his mother's door;
Recedes the dream of triumphant return.

Bones turn brittle with each winter's chill,
And as the snow lays its switch on the soul,

Memory, like leaves, rots underfoot.

And so the passion for rhythm in dens,
Wherein to drown prickly thoughts of Home
In pint after pint of imported brew.

all because i loved you

once, i wrote with the irreverence of youth
and the fire of a heart burning to ash
i plucked words like faggots from blazing coal
on the anvil of exile i hammered sorrow into verse
the burden of your suffering tore poetry from my flesh
on the night of your hanging there was dust in my lines
i aimed for song yet could not find
a single dry eye in the house

i marked the fourteen stations of the cross
but your death has killed my verse
each day i wake on the hour to mourn
and i feel like a wanderer in a city without lights
passion escapes in the fog and words crumble
at my touch and my throat feels like a concrete floor
the power of tears has deserted me

i walk through the streets of this forbidding town
searching for faces that i used to know
your memory is like a faded picture in the pocket

here and there i hear your name
like the distant crack of a whip
and there's a dull pain where the scars remain
i recall your stubbornness, and the ring of blood
on your wrist and i embrace this cold
that severed you from me

once, i howled with the rage of a bard
there was epiphany in the pain
and all because i loved you
now i claw the walls for the naked word
my lines are a hollow sepulcher
ready for the final dust
silence claims us at last.

Reflection

or Sonnet for A.

~~Of tAnd~~ The distance that grew between them
Neither had anticipated ~~True,~~
Though one of them had mentioned
A deep ~~feeling sense~~ feeling of desertion
And the other often spoken ~~often often spoken~~
Of the dangerous power of ~~love~~ passion
Yet, neither had once predicted
~~That summer could yield so resolutely~~
~~To the chill of autumn frost or~~
That a river could dry so quickly
Or summer yield so resolutely
To the chill of autumn frost
Of their shared past ~~little~~ naught survives
It seems, but this one last resolve
That neither blame nor hate ~~shall~~
Should ever come between them.

Conversation

And where ~~is that accent from~~?
Is that accent from?
He asked politely.
Biafra, I replied,
~~that's where I'm from~~That's where I'm from.
Biafra, he ~~said after much thought~~ repeated
And pondered the word awhile. ~~I know~~
I'm sure I've heard ~~of~~
Of that nation before.
It's not a nation
Sir, I corrected
~~It's only in the imagination~~Only a notion
In the imagination.
Well, he politely replied ~~politely~~
After further reflection,
There are no nations;
Only the imagination.
The mirror is a window.
~~That~~ It offers a glimpse
Of where ~~you~~ we're from

But cannot return.
We're all travelers
On this endless road
Condemned to roam
Without repose.

The Sadness Descends Again

The sadness descends again
Sodden like a sheet of ice
Yet, somehow through the shawl
A smile, stubborn as a thumb

Pries its way to life
A cotyledon of light
Defies the night.

Offering

Here's to the native gods wandering unheralded
Here's to the naked gods wandering the plains
Here's to the maize god, the potato god, the cotton god
Here's to the spirits of the premature dead

Here's to the million souls loitering unatoned
Here's to the unacknowledged, abandoned & forgotten
Here's to the Prophet as he faces the firing squad
Here's to the unborn & the empty tomb

Here's your three lobes
Here your piece of chalk
Here's your palm frond
And your fresh chicken blood.

Almanac

February and April brought sorrow and pain.
May is the month of burial and memorial.
March went by with mourning in its wake.
Spring came late right around Lent.

The early bud withered on the frozen limb,
While draft sipped through the shuttered pane.
Shall I toss a coin on the pyre for your journey,
Or open the levee when the ashes come in?

Prayer

O, glorious day, be my renewal
Be my search and recovery
Sand lost in sand under the dunes
Be my beacon and turning sign
Restless sun, be my return
Be my ascent and break my fall.

There Was a Country

The hummingbird lies in the brushes
His heart impaled to earth in the brushes

The songbird lies where his fresh blood
Mingled with the soil and dirt in the brushes

The songbird cries unsung in the brushes
And now his blood trickles through the ravines

And the stream becomes a river
And the river becomes a waterfall

And his blood becomes one with the blood
Of the mother and child, and the thousand and one

Score who lie under the sodden soil in the brushes

The blood of the songbird cries through
The night and he would not be consoled for

There was a country

And on its altar, the heart of a sunbird, freshly cut
And a flag with half of a yellow sun

The bones of the songbird lie in the brushes
Waiting for the Second Coming.

Memory

Who can tell the depth of my loss?
What tool or sophisticated instrument
Can read or take full measure of the
Length and breadth of our inner pain?

Faint in the howl of the Harmattan wind
The voice of the poet in the wilderness rings
Do not forget the blood that was shed
Nor the anguish of the living dead

Speak the word, then
That the children may hear
That all who forget are condemned to die
Not one, but a thousand and one deaths.

The Curse

From every hamlet, they came
From every dialect and clan
They stood in a great multitude
And they read out one by one
The names of the innocent dead
And for each name that was read
They put a curse on the nation
For every drop of innocent blood
Another curse, world without end.

Seven Stations of the Cross

for Esiaba Irobi

From Leeds to Liverpool
Liverpool to London
London to New York
New York to Towson
Towson to Athens
The beaconer takes his bow in Berlin
And the exile becomes Myth

Seven Stations of the Cross

I leave to live, said he
I e*xit to exist.*

The Healing

Neither silver nor gold have I, said she
But such as I have shall I give to thee:

Rise up and walk.

And she took him by the right hand
And lifted him up.

Immediately, his feet and ankle bones
Received strength.

Pledge

After Ruth 1:16

Henceforth shall I leave you
And turn my back on you
And where you dwell I shall not
For your people are not my people
And your god is not my god.

www.ingramcontent.com/pod-product-compliance
Lightning Source LLC
La Vergne TN
LVHW090941080826
845145LV00003B/845

* 9 7 8 0 9 8 4 8 6 9 5 1 0 *